PIRATES AND PRIVATEERS THE GOLDEN AGE OF PIRATES

CHAPTER ONE THE GOLDEN AGE OF PIRATES

The golden age of pirates and piracy on the high seas 1650-1726

It's a common misconception that pirates were romantic renegades who lived on islands and sailed the open sea in search of treasure. In reality, they were brutal criminals who preyed on merchant ships and used their loot to finance empires. While many pirates did end up residing in the Caribbean, others made their home in areas as far-flung as the Red Sea or Indonesia. And while some had black flags fluttering from their masts, many others flew red or yellow ones.

Piracy was not limited to the Caribbean.

PIRACY WAS NOT LIMITED to the Caribbean. Pirates were active in the Mediterranean, the Atlantic and the Indian Ocean, as well as in the Red Sea and Persian Gulf, China Sea and Pacific.

- The Mediterranean was a popular hunting ground for pirates because of its trade routes that connected Europe with North Africa and Asia. By attacking merchant ships on these routes, pirates could easily find rich pickings. In addition to plundering cargo they also kidnapped passengers who were then held for ransom or sold into slavery.

• During this period there were numerous pirate bases located off both coasts of Africa which enabled them to attack ships traveling between Europe and Asia without having to return home if they failed to find any prizes worth seizing; these bases became established bases for buccaneers during their raids against Spanish colonies such as Cuba and Puerto Rico.

Barbary corsairs used their treasure to finance the Ottoman Empire.

THE BARBARY CORSAIRS were Muslim pirates who preyed on European shipping in the Mediterranean. They were funded by the Ottoman Empire, and they were based in North Africa. However, the term "Barbary Corsairs" isn't restricted to those operating from the coast of Algeria—the name was applied to any pirate operating out of a place called "Barbaria."

Pirates were not romantic renegades.

THERE ARE A LOT OF misconceptions about pirates. Another common misconception is that pirates were romantic renegades, but this couldn't be farther from the truth.

Pirates were ruthless and cruel—their violence was not only directed at their enemies, but also toward anyone who got in their way. They would kill anyone who threatened their way of life or stood between them and treasure—even if it was just one passenger on board a ship they captured! That being said, many people did live through encounters with pirates and lived to tell the tale (more on this later).

In short: don't believe everything you hear about pirates being heroic or romantic figures just because modern day films portray them as such! Most of what Hollywood has told us about these men isn't true—they were criminals who took over ships by force (or sometimes even without any battles) simply because they could get away with it; there's nothing heroic about breaking into someone else's home without permission is there?

Jamaican pirates were eventually expelled from their base in Port Royal by a massive earthquake.

IN 1692, JAMAICA WAS hit by a massive earthquake. It was the second-largest earthquake ever recorded in history and caused over 2,000 deaths—including many pirates who were living at Port Royal.

The quake destroyed much of the city and left it unable to sustain its economy as a pirate haven anymore. The capital was moved to Kingston, which is still the island's largest city today.

Pirate crews were not democratic.

THE WORD "DEMOCRACY" comes from the Greek words demos and kratos, which literally mean "people power." The idea is that everyone in a society has equal rights and responsibilities. In practice, this means citizens have a say in their government's actions through voting or other forms of participation.

Pirate crews were not like this at all—they did not have any kind of democratic structure or system of governance. There was no election process for captains or crew members to rise through the ranks either; pirates simply took what they wanted when they wanted it, whether it was treasure or booty (the goods taken from captured ships).

Pirates also didn't answer to anyone above them on land or at sea—they weren't forced to follow laws as long as they stayed far away from ports where authorities could enforce them.

Pirate ships were not identical to merchant ships.

MOST PIRATE SHIPS WERE smaller than merchant vessels, and they had more speed and agility. This was because pirates did not carry heavy cargo like a regular merchant ship would carry, so the ship could be smaller. Also, the crew of a pirate ship was usually much smaller than that of a merchant vessel, because pirates needed only to be able to sail their vessel effectively. Because these ships carried less weight, they were lighter and could move faster through the water.

Pirate ships also did not have cabins for captains or sails on top of them (which was common among other kinds of large seafaring vessels). Sailors often slept below deck in hammocks instead of beds; food was stored in lockers, sailors bathed with seawater rather than fresh water; there were no toilets aboard pirate vessels—instead it was common practice for men who needed to relieve themselves on long voyages at sea simply climb overboard into their small boats anchored nearby!

Most pirate ships had black flags, but there were exceptions.

MOST PIRATE SHIPS HAD black flags, but there were exceptions. The most famous of these is the red flag that flew on Captain Henry Morgan's ship during his raid on Panama in 1671. The red flag meant no quarter—anyone who resisted was to be killed or enslaved without mercy.

Pirates sometimes flew different flags depending on who they were attacking. For example, if they encountered a Spanish galleon carrying its own cargo as well as a treasure shipment from Peru or Mexico, they would hoist their usual black pirate flag and then use another one with an image of a woman holding a palm branch in her right hand and reaching out toward three castles flying Spanish flags beneath her left arm (this was meant to represent Spain's power over Portugal). This second flag let everyone know not only that this Spanish vessel was carrying booty but also that it belonged to someone other than Spain itself; thus it could be taken by force without breaking any international laws concerning property rights over cargo owned by other countries' citizens traveling across open waters aboard vessels registered with their governments instead of private companies like those owned by merchants seeking protection from piracy through common carriers such as Lloyd's of London."

Some pirates and privateers were women.

YOU MAY BE SURPRISED to learn that some pirates and privateers were women. In fact, they were rare, but they did exist. They include:

- Mary Read (1690-1721)
- Anne Bonny (circa 1689-1720)

Mary was a pirate who disguised herself as a man to board ships and steal their treasure. She became friends with Anne Bonny, who was the lover of the pirate Calico Jack Rackham. Both Mary and Anne used to dress like men because it was easier for them to get work on ships if they were men instead of women. If you saw these women walking down the street in your town today, you might think they were just regular girls out for a stroll.

Piracy on the high seas was a brutal business and pirates were ruthless with their prey.

PIRATES WEREN'T THE most compassionate people on the high seas, and they would not hesitate to kill if it meant a profit. They tortured captives for information, especially those who had money or goods that pirates could take from them. Pirates also killed for fun; torturing captives was seen as a sport by some pirates.

What's more, pirates would kill anyone who tried to escape from them—even captives who had surrendered before capture.

So, as you can see, there was a lot of piracy in the early 1700s. We can't say for sure whether it was the "golden age of pirates" or not (especially since we don't know what other golden ages there might have been), but it definitely seems like the time period had more than its share of sea-going outlaws. This era marked a turning point in history when nations built navies with an eye towards protecting their trade routes rather than dominating others militarily—and pirates were able to thrive because they were still able to prey on the merchant ships that sailed through dangerous waters without support from any government.

CHAPTER TWO SIR FRANCIS DRAKE

Sir Francis Drake world famous pirate

T he life of Sir Francis Drake has been the subject of legends since his death. He was a privateer, navigator, explorer, and politician – but most importantly he was a pirate.

Early Life

FRANCIS DRAKE WAS BORN in 1540 in Tavistock, Devon, England. His father was a Protestant farmer and his mother was a widow who remarried another farmer. At age 12, Drake began to go on sailing voyages with his stepfather's fleet of ships. In 1569 he led an attack against the Spanish settlement of Nombre de Dios (near modern-day Colón) in Panama. The Spanish town had become rich through trade with Central America and South America, but Drake's raid ruined the town's economy by stealing its gold bullion shipments and burning all its ships at sea so they could not return home or leave port again until new ships were built to take their place; this caused a great financial loss for Spain as well as depriving it of precious metals used by colonists elsewhere around the world."

England and the New World

ENGLAND WAS A POWERFUL country in the 16th century. It had a strong navy and was involved in many wars with Spain. Spain was a powerful empire at the time, with colonies in Central and South America (called "the New World"). The Spanish navy was also very strong, so it wasn't easy for England to attack their colonies there.

Double crosses and war

DRAKE WAS A PRIVATEER and politician. As a sailor, he commanded three ships in the service of Queen Elizabeth I—the Pelican, Golden Hind, and Pelican again—and became the first Englishman to circumnavigate the globe (1577-1580). He sailed to South America, where his fleet captured several Spanish ships and plundered their cargoes.

After Drake's death from dysentery at sea near Puerto Rico in 1596 (he was buried at sea), his survivors returned home with great riches taken from Spanish ships. The queen knighted him posthumously for his achievements as an explorer, pirate hunter, and politician who had served her well during her years on the throne.

Francis Drake was a brilliant commander, navigator, and seaman, who changed the course of European history.

DRAKE'S FIRST NOTABLE exploit came in 1573 when he sailed to America with his friend Sir John Hawkins to attack Spanish ships near Florida. After being badly wounded in battle, Drake led a retreat from Panama that turned into a round-the-world voyage that included his capture of Cuzco in Peru. In 1577 he returned home to be rewarded by Queen Elizabeth I with a knighthood and command over an expedition against Spain's colonies in the West Indies.

Francis Drake was born in 1540 in Devonshire, England.

HIS PARENTS WERE PROTESTANT farmers who were forced to flee England during the reign of Queen Mary I (also known as "Bloody Mary"). Although it is not known for certain, some historians think that Francis Drake may have been a sailor before he became a pirate and privateer.

He left home when he was about 20 years old because his father wanted him to attend university. He also had an argument with his brother John about religion; Francis believed in Protestantism while John followed Catholicism - which was at that time illegal under English law!

It's a good thing that Drake's parents were Protestant, since they were forced to flee England during the reign of Queen Mary I. This Catholic queen persecuted Protestants and tried to turn England back into a Catholic country.

The Drake family returned to England after Mary died and her half-sister Elizabeth took over. Francis Drake was born in 1540 or 1541 in Tavistock, Devon. His father was Edmund Drake (a mariner) and his mother was Elizabeth Sydenham; both had been farmers.

The family returned to England after Mary's death.

AFTER MARY'S DEATH and the defeat of the Spanish Armada, Drake's family was forced to leave England. They returned after Elizabeth's accession in 1558, when Sir Francis's father was granted a coat-of-arms and his son became captain of Plymouth. Sir Francis Drake had married Mary Newman around 1567 and they had five sons who survived into adulthood: James Gascoigne; John Drake; Nicholas (who died young); Benjamin Gillingham (1588–1655), who made his fortune trading with Virginia; and George Lelande (1589–1625), who also traded with Virginia but later went bankrupt.

In 1562 Drake was appointed master of a ship that traded between England and Portugal. The following year he sailed to Guinea where he was involved in several trading ventures before returning home via Madeira Island off the coast of Portugal.

Drake's father died when he was young and his mother

remarried another farmer with a salt-works and small fleet of ships that sailed to France and Spain.

THEY LIVED NEAR PLYMOUTH in Devon, England. Drake went to sea at the age of 16, serving as an apprentice on a ship headed for the West Indies.

Drake worked with his stepfather's fleet as a boy and began sailing out of privateering expeditions out of Plymouth, England in 1563.

DRAKE BEGAN TO WORK with his stepfather's fleet as a boy, and he began sailing out of Plymouth shortly after. This was a period when England was at war with Spain (the Spanish Armada), and Drake joined with other privateers in their attacks on enemy ships. Like pirates, privateers were not sanctioned by the government but rather operated on their own accord with the permission of their monarchs in order to attack hostile targets.

His first major expedition took place in 1569 when he led an attack against the Spanish settlement of Nombre de Dios in Panama.

HE WAS THE FIRST ENGLISHMAN to attack Nombre de Dios and succeeded in stealing a large amount of gold from the Spanish.

King Philip II of Spain was furious over this attack, but Drake was not afraid to tangle with him again and again.

He was knighted by Queen Elizabeth I in 1581 for his incredible success as both a privateer against the Spanish and as a politician for the English Parliament.

HE WAS ALSO KNOWN AS a privateer, buccaneer, corsair, and mariner.

He continued to lead attacks against the Spanish until he died of dysentery at sea near Puerto Rico in 1596.

AS A PIRATE, FRANCIS Drake was the most famous Englishman of his time. His attacks on Spanish ships were so destructive that he earned a name for himself and became the focus of many stories and myths.

A pirate also called a corsair or buccaneer was a privateer.

YOU'RE ONE STEP AHEAD of most people who have heard about the life and adventures of Sir Francis Drake. If not, allow me to explain: A pirate is a person who robs ships at sea. A privateer is someone who takes part in acts of war on behalf of his country. During this period in history, when Spain ruled much of Europe and had colonies around the world (including what are now Mexico and South America), it was common for countries like England and France to recruit privateers—paid soldiers—to attack Spanish shipping and settlements along their coastlines.

The most famous pirates were probably Blackbeard and William Kidd.

BLACKBEARD WAS A REAL pirate who sailed the Caribbean in the early 1700s. He had a reputation for cruelty and violence, and his real name was Edward Teach.

William Kidd was an Irish-born sailor who became infamous for being a pirate in the Indian Ocean around 1695 to 1701, but he later settled down and became an official privateer for Britain's King William III (the same king who ruled over England when Shakespeare wrote Macbeth).

Pirate ships were usually armed with cannons, guns, and other weapons.

CANNONS AND GUNS WERE used to attack enemy ships. They could also be used to defend against attacks from other ships, or to defend ports and towns. Pirate ships often carried several cannons, which were very heavy and difficult to move around. Cannons had a wide range of sizes and shapes, but they all fired projectiles such as metal balls or stone boulders. These weapons could cause great damage in battle if they hit their targets accurately enough!

Pirates are a part of history that captured the imaginations of people for centuries. Pirates were often romanticized as heroes, and even though they were criminals, they were seen as rebels against authority. They have been a part of popular culture for centuries.

Life was hard on both sides, but today's historians can still learn a lot from studying their lives and times.

CHAPTER THREE EDWARD TEACH AKA BLACK BEARD THE PIRATE

Blackbeard was one of the most successful pirates in history. There were too many other pirates in Jamaica so he sailed north and settled in North Carolina where he made his home base. He attacked many merchant ships sailing from Jamaica and the South Seas, earning himself a reputation as one of the cruelest pirates who ever lived.

Blackbeard was one of the most famous pirates of the golden age.

HE EARNED HIS NICKNAME "The Lord High Admiral of the Navy of the Caribbean." His favorite drinking game was to pour rum over a hot shovel, then stick the shovel into a pot of boiling water.

He was born in Bristol, England around 1680.

HIS FATHER WAS JOHN Teach, a privateer who sailed for the British Navy during the War of Spanish Succession. His mother was Rebecca Anne Teach and she had one other son named James. He also had a sister named Katherine who was born in 1703 when Edward was around 23 years old.

THERE WERE TOO MANY pirates in Jamaica. Blackbeard realized that if he stayed there, he would be caught by the British Navy or the Spanish Navy (or both). So he sailed north to North Carolina, which was a good place for hiding because it had lots of islands and narrow creeks where ships could hide.

Blackbeard was born Edward Teach but little is known about his early years.

THE EXACT DATE OF HIS birth is unknown, but it is believed that he was born in Bristol around 1680. Later on, he adopted the name Blackbeard and became notorious for his beard which had been combed into several tails and tied with black ribbons. After making a name for himself as a pirate captain, Blackbeard began using this nickname to terrify his victims and make them believe that he was actually Satan himself because of his long beard.

He spent time in Jamaica, which was a popular place for pirates to live.

IT WAS A SAFE HAVEN for pirates, helping them hide from the law. They could get supplies and information in Jamaica.

He attacked many merchant ships sailing from Jamaica and the South Seas.

IT WAS COMMON FOR TEACH to light fuses in his beard and terrorize passing vessels. This was a trick he used while sailing with Anne Bonny, who would be one of the first female pirates to join his crew.

The ship he used to terrorize boats had 40 guns on it, which were enough to scare most merchant ships into surrendering without a fight.

ONE OF BLACKBEARD'S most famous tactics was to light fuses in his beard. As the story goes, he would wear a thick black wig and light it on fire before going into battle. This would scare his enemies so much that they would surrender their ships without a fight.

Another way that Blackbeard scared people was by walking around with pistols in each hand and swinging them around at his sides as he walked. He also liked bragging about how many men he had killed during his career as a pirate and letting everyone know that he "would kill" anyone who crossed him.

His ship had 40 guns, which scared a lot of people into surrendering their ships without a fight.

A LOT OF PEOPLE WERE scared into surrendering their ships without a fight because of this. It was called the Queen Anne's Revenge and it was one of the biggest pirate ships in history!

Blackbeard (who also went by Edward Teach) was a very successful pirate because he had such a powerful ship and crew.

The story of Blackbeard the pirate is full of legends and exaggerations but one thing is true - he was very successful at getting treasure from merchant ships

BLACKBEARD WAS A PIRATE who earned his nickname "The Lord High Admiral of the Navy of the Caribbean." He is often claimed to have had a beard that stretched down to his waist, but this may not be true.

Blackbeard's pirate ship could hold up to 90 people and he used it to attack merchant ships near Bermuda, Jamaica and North Carolina between 1717-1718. Blackbeard wore an eye patch over one eye because a surgeon cut out his left eye when he was young.

He became a very successful pirate with a huge beard. The story goes that he would light his face on fire with gunpowder and then put out the flames by drinking rum from one of his two flasks, which were hidden in his beard. This made him look like some kind of monster or demon to people who saw him approach their ships at night! To others who were watching from far away though, it seemed like Blackbeard had just found a way to breathe fire—which is pretty cool too!

BLACKBEARD'S FLAGSHIP, which he named the Queen Anne's Revenge, was a third rate warship. This meant that it was armed with 40 cannons and had a crew of 140 men. After being captured by Blackbeard, the ship sailed on for about two years before being sunk in 1718 by an Englishman named Robert Maynard (who later founded the town of Norfolk).

The Queen Anne's Revenge was built in 1696 by John Haskett at Deptford Dockyard near London, England. It was originally called Concorde and belonged to King William III of Great Britain (who also owned another famous ship called Victory).

Blackbeard was a scoundrel who earned his fortune by stealing from other ships.

HE WAS JUST ONE OF many pirates, privateers and buccaneers who sailed the seas during that time period. He's well-known today because he had a reputation for being cruel and violent, which made him notorious among sailors.

BLACKBEARD'S FAVORITE drinking game involved pouring rum over an iron shovel hot enough to make steam come out of it, then putting that shovel into a pot full of boiling water. The liquid from the heated metal would drip onto paper below as he held his face above the pot to catch it with his mouth (don't try this at home).

BLACKBEARD'S MAIN SHIPS were the Queen Anne's Revenge, a frigate, and the Adventure Galley, a sloop.

The Queen Anne's Revenge was originally a Spanish ship that Blackbeard captured in 1717 and turned into his flagship for several years. The ship also carried some of Blackbeard's own cannons and had accommodations for up to 300 crew members when fully loaded with supplies.

The Adventure Galley was captured by Blackbeard shortly after he took over the Queen Anne's Revenge in 1717 as well. It was originally named La Concorde but renamed to Adventure Galley before being given over to Blackbeard's pirate crew. This smaller ship usually carried around 90 men aboard her during their voyages under his command.

Edward Teach or Blackbeard was an infamous pirate in the Caribbean during the Golden Age of Piracy. He was born on November 22, 1680, and died in battle with Lt. Robert Maynard in Ocracoke Inlet on December 6, 1718. His ship the Queen Anne's Revenge is now being excavated in Beaufort Inlet.

CHAPTER FOUR SIR HENRY MORGAN

The life of Sir Henry Morgan Pirate

Sir Henry Morgan was born in 1635 at Llanrumney, Monmouthshire, South Wales. His father had a farm about a mile from Cardiff and young Henry spent his boyhood here. We know little of Morgan's early life except that he became a seaman and took part in the buccaneering expeditions that were led by Admiral Christopher Myngs (1625-1666). The buccaneers were a lawless band of adventurers engaged in raiding Spanish colonies. In 1663 Governor Thomas Modyford sent Captain Henry Morgan on an expedition to Puerto Principe, Cuba. With 27 ships and 2,000 men, Morgan burned the town of Puerto Principe and then defeated a superior Spanish force on 27 April 1663. The following year he captured San Francisco de Campeche (now known as Campeche) on the coast of Yucatan. On 3 March 1668 Morgan was appointed commander-in-chief in Jamaica."

Sir Henry Morgan, admiral of the buccaneers and the most famous of all the privateers of the West Indies, was born in 1635 at Llanrumney, Monmouthshire, South Wales.

AS A YOUNG MAN, HENRY'S father was a farmer. He had a farm in Wales, where he grew crops and raised livestock. His mother was the farmer's wife.

In his early years, Henry Morgan spent most of his time working on the family farm. He learned how to work with animals like horses and cows; he also learned how to plant different kinds of vegetables like potatoes or carrots in the ground so they could grow into food for people to eat later on during winter months when there wasn't any fresh fruit available yet because it takes longer than one year before plants start producing fruit.

WHEN HE WAS FOURTEEN years old he went to school at Cowbridge under the Rev. Francis Clark, who afterwards became vicar of St. Mary's Church and Dean of Llandaff. Mr Clark taught his pupils Latin and Greek by means of the 'Grammatica Latina' published by Dr Martin Rinkart (1586-1656) who had been rector at Strasbourg University before coming to England as chaplain to King James I in 1619 (see illustration).

We know little of Morgan's early life except that he became a seaman and took part in the buccaneering expeditions that were led by Admiral Christopher Myngs (1625-1666).

MORGAN HAD TWO WIVES. One, Elizabeth Burnaby, was the daughter of a former governor of Jamaica who died during the great fire at Port Royal. The other, Martha Caroline Taylor, whom he married around 1699, was the sister-in-law of Sir James Almont and widow of Captain Henry Pimbutter; she died in 1717 at Port Royal. Morgan fathered some six children with his first wife. The name of only one child has been recorded: Catherine Morgan married Francis Bannister at Kingston on December 23rd 1678; her date of birth is unknown but she must have been born before this date because her father had moved to Jamaica by then and she could not have traveled there without him or someone else taking care of her (obviously not possible if you're an infant).

The buccaneers were a lawless band of adventurers engaged in raiding Spanish colonies.

WELL, NOT EXACTLY. The word "buccaneer" actually comes from the French word boucan, which is a wooden frame used by hunters to smoke meat over an open fire. The term was coined by the French government to describe pirates who raided settlements on Caribbean islands and preyed on shipping along the coasts of Central America and northern South America.

The buccaneers were not a lawless band of adventurers. Rather than operating as an organized force with its own command structure and rules, they were independent bands of individuals who came together when convenient—and parted ways when needed or convenient once again. Their ranks included escaped slaves, runaway sailors, deserters from European armies or navies (including those of Spain), thieves and criminals—basically anyone willing to live outside society's rules because it suited them better than living within society's rules would have done!

In 1663 Governor Thomas Modyford sent Captain Henry Morgan on an expedition to Puerto Principe, Cuba.

IN APRIL 1663, MORGAN was sent to Cuba with 27 ships and 2,000 men. He burned the town of Puerto Principe and defeated a superior Spanish force on 27 April 1663.

WHEN MORGAN'S CAREER as a pirate began, he was appointed commander-in-chief of the maritime forces in Jamaica.

The following year he captured San Francisco de Campeche (now known as Campeche) on the coast of Yucatan.

CAMPECHE WAS ONE OF the biggest cities in Yucatan at the time. In 1669, Morgan's fleet captured it by surprise and looted the treasure ships anchored in its harbor. They also burned down the town and took captive many people.

The governor of Campeche was forced to pay a ransom to Morgan for his release.

On 3 March 1668 Morgan was appointed commander-in-chief in Jamaica.

HE ALSO SERVED AS LIEUTENANT governor from 1668 to 1671, when he was promoted to admiral and appointed governor from 1674 until his death in 1688.

Although his career as a freebooter came to an end in 1672 when he was made lieutenant governor of Jamaica with the rank of admiral, he continued to fight the Spaniards until war between England and Spain broke out in 1655.

MORGAN WAS APPOINTED lieutenant governor of Jamaica in 1672. He governed with great vigor and energy, seeing that justice was done impartially and quickly. He also encouraged agriculture and trade, but did not forget defense: he built up Fort Charles at Port Royal, and established other fortifications around the island.

HENRY MORGAN WAS A privateer and commander of the buccaneers. He is best remembered for his exploits in the Caribbean and southern North America during the 1660s.

CHAPTER FIVE WILLIAM KIDD

William Kidd was a Scottish sailor who became famous in the early 1700s. He is famous because he was accused of being a pirate and was tried and hanged for it.

Kidd was born in Dundee, Scotland around 1645. He went to sea in his early teens and became captain at the age of 20. In 1689, he married a widow with five children who already had three sons from her first marriage; they had one daughter together named Sarah.

In 1695 as part of what has been called "The War Against France" (which lasted from 1689-1697) William Kidd was commissioned by the British government to raid French ships on the high seas using letters of marque issued by King William III which allowed him to capture enemy vessels without being subject to prosecution if caught doing so. At first he did quite well but then things started going poorly when one ship under his command sunk due to bad weather conditions off Madagascar Island with all its crew lost except two men who were taken prisoner by natives; another ship under his command was wrecked off Africa's east coast while trying unsuccessfully yet again at attacking more French vessels; upon arriving back home safely again after this latest failure though instead of being praised for surviving these mishaps despite odds stacked against him Captain Kidd found himself facing charges brought against him by some former colleagues claiming that he'd been cheating them out of their share fees earned through previous voyages involving similar missions for England - even though there had never been any proof offered during these earlier journeys suggesting wrongdoing existed anywhere along.

William Kidd was born in Dundee, Scotland around 1645. His parents were Robert and Margaret Kidd. He had a brother named John and a sister named Ann.

William Kidd grew up in Dundee as an apprentice to his father who was an Episcopal minister there. In 1689 he moved to New York City where he became a seaman and started sailing around the world. He married Sarah Bradley Cox Oortmandt around 1690, but she died eight months later while they were living in Boston Massachusetts due to complications from childbirth (she gave birth to their son Thomas).

In 1695 William Kidd became captain of his own ship called "Adventure Galley". The ship was purchased by investors who wanted him to go on voyages searching for pirates so that they could get revenge against them because numerous ships had been attacked by these criminals.

William Kidd went to sea in his early teens.

HE HAD BEEN WORKING as a sailor from an early age, and by the time he was 16 years old, he was working on ships that sailed between Scotland and England.

Kidd was a skilled sailor—he even became famous for navigating around icebergs. But he also had a reputation for being bad-tempered. According to legend, this may have been due to side effects of drinking too much rum.

In 1689 he married a widow called Sarah Oort. She came from a rich Dutch family, which helped him to become more important as a businessman in New York City.

KIDD WAS NOT THE ONLY pirate to work in New York City. At that time, there were some other pirates who also used to live in or around New York City because it was an important port and they could get help from people in New York City.

In 1694, he got the chance to captain a ship called the Adventure Galley. The job offered good pay and a high rank but was also dangerous. Privateers were ships that were given permission to attack enemy ships during the war. They were usually small, fast, and well-armed, making them ideal for attacking other smaller vessels such as merchantmen or fishing boats.

The Adventure Galley was just that—a pirate ship with a license to terrorize anyone foolish enough to get in its way.

William Kidd became an important businessman in New York City by marrying Sarah Oort, who came from a rich Dutch family.

WILLIAM KIDD IS AN important figure in history. He is famous because he was accused of being a pirate and was tried and hanged. We hope this has given you some insight into his life and the time in which he lived.

CHAPTER SIX GRACE O'MALLEY PIRATE QUEEN

G race O'Malley is one of the most well known female pirates of all time. She was a tough fighter who wasn't afraid to stand up for her family's rights. Her life story has been retold in books and movies, but there are still many things you might not know about this Irish warrior queen. Here are facts about Ireland's very own pirate queen:

Grace O'Malley is said to have been fearless, and she was a tough fighter who wasn't afraid to stand up for her family's rights.

IN THE 15TH CENTURY, pirates ruled the seas. These men were fearless and they weren't afraid to stand up for their rights. Grace O'Malley was one of those pirates. She was a woman who spent her days sailing around Ireland in her ship chasing people down and stealing from them as well as leading raids on English settlements along the coast of Ireland.

Grace O'Malley stands out as an important figure because she lived at a time when women were expected to stay home and not get involved in politics or sailing around fighting people on ships.

Like many women of her time, O'Malley was married off by her family to ensure that a wealthy clan would be joining their own. Marriage was a way to secure alliances between clans, ensure property would be passed down from one generation to the next, and bring wealth and influence into the family. In Ireland at this time, it was not uncommon for young girls to be married as soon as they reached puberty or even earlier—sometimes as young as eight years old!

It's also important to remember that O'Malley, while her given name was Gráinne Mhaol, had another name as well. That other name was Gráinne Ní Mháille, and it translates to "Bald Grainne," or "grainne of the tonsured head." The reason for this nickname is that O'Malley's father was the chieftain of the Ó Máille clan during his time on land. However, he found himself exiled from Ireland when he was accused of killing another man in a violent dispute over land rights. During this time where her father lived on an island off the west coast of Ireland called Clare Island (and later moved to County Mayo), O'Malley learned how to fight with her fists and how to use weapons like polearms such as spears and swords—skills she would use later in life when she became known for leading pirate excursions against foreign ships in search for gold or other valuable cargo.

The O'Malleys were a noble clan from Ireland.

ONE OF IRELAND'S MOST celebrated pirates and privateers, she had a big impact on history that has been lost to time. Here's what we know about her:

- She was from an Irish noble family called O'Malley
- The O'Malleys were from the West Coast of Ireland (Connemara)
- They also lived in Galway, Mayo, and other places along that coast

Although Grace married twice in her life, neither marriage was happy.

MARRIAGE WAS A BUSINESS transaction among noble families in Ireland at that time and arranged marriages were common. The marriages weren't always made out of love; they were much more often made to strengthen alliances between clans and keep the family property within the family.

When O'Malley's first husband died at sea, she took over control of his fleet and became a pirate.

GRACE O'MALLEY WAS an Irish pirate queen who lived from about 1530 to 1603. She was a successful businesswoman and mother, but she is most famous for leading her own fleet of ships as if they were an army.

She had a strong will and was very independent—she didn't care what others thought of her because she knew that the only way to achieve success was by working hard and not relying on anyone else.

You might have heard that when her first husband, Donal O'Flaherty, died, Grace cut her hair short as an outward sign of her grief. This is true—but it's not clear whether she did this because she mourned for him or to make herself less attractive to other men.

O'Malley is one of the most well known female pirates of all-time.

CHAPTER SEVEN ANNE BONNY

There is perhaps no more famous female pirate than Anne Bonny, who captained a ship with her lover Calico Jack. She was an unlikely pirate, born in Ireland to a poor weaver and his wife. Though she had little education and no formal training as a sailor, Bonny embraced life at sea as an opportunity for adventure and self-discovery. In the early 1720s she rose through the ranks of Caribbean pirate captains until she reached her peak with Rackham—by this time known by the name Charles Vane—and Mary Read (a woman who dressed up like a man).

During the Golden Age of Piracy, a female pirate captured imaginations in a way no other female had before.

WHEN YOU THINK OF PIRATES, you probably imagine a male. But Anne Bonny was the exception to this rule, becoming one of only two female pirates known by name during the Golden Age (1660-1700) and the only woman ever hanged for piracy in that era.

Both her father and grandfather were pirates as well as smugglers; it was not uncommon for children in this family line to be raised with firebrand traits that would eventually lead them towards their own pirating lifestyle. Anne grew up in Jamaica where she spent most of her childhood among freebooters. She first met John "Calico Jack" Rackham when she was 15 years old – he was 22 at the time – and they married shortly thereafter.[1]

In the early 18th century, a young Irish girl named Mary Read was born to a poor weaver and his wife.

SHE WAS BORN IN 1690 in England, where her parents lived in poverty. Her father worked as a weaver and her mother stayed at home with the children.

Mary had three brothers: John, James and Peter. In those days, it wasn't uncommon for families to have many children because they needed more hands to help support them financially.

As good as her disguise proved to be, it could not protect her from the dangers of sea life forever.

ANNE WAS NOT CAUGHT for a long time. However, her luck ran out when she became pregnant with Calico Jack's child (a boy).

Now pregnant with Calico Jack's child, Anne Bonny returned to Charles Towne where she was arrested, and gave birth to their son in August 1721.

AFTER HER RETURN TO Charles Towne and giving birth to their son in August 1721, Anne Bonny was released from prison due to being pregnant and returned to Nassau with Calico Jack. However, he soon ran afoul of a local pirate-hunter named Woodes Rogers who had been appointed governor of the Bahamas by King George I of England five months earlier.

Soon after Rogers' appointment as governor, he began an aggressive campaign against pirates operating in the area. He set up an outpost at Nassau Harbour and issued pardons to all those who surrendered their pirate ships, weapons and loot without resistance or bloodshed. However, when Calico Jack refused his pardon offer on 24 October 1718, he ordered him arrested along with his crew. They were put on trial for piracy at St James's Palace (London).

In September 1720, an informant told Charles Towne's governor about Rackham's whereabouts

DURING THE SUMMER OF 1720, a man named Robert Deal brought information to Charles Towne's governor about Rackham's whereabouts. He claimed that he had been captured by Jamaica-based pirates and forced to join their crew. One night he slipped away from them while they were sleeping and ran into another ship that was anchored nearby. Though he didn't know who they were or where they were going, Deal claimed that the captain must have told him something because the next day his ship was attacked by another vessel whose crew was led by (Bonny) and Mary Read.

Deal told this story to Governor Johnson during an interview at his home on Johns Island with several other witnesses present. Johnson asked him why he'd waited so long before coming forward with this information; Deal replied that he had initially feared retribution from Rackham when they met again in Port Royal since Rackham had always treated him well in the past despite knowing what Deal did for a living (in other words: because he wasn't afraid of being caught).

Though she was let off due to her pregnancy, Calico Jack was put on trial and hanged on November 1720.

THE BABY WAS BORN BUT taken away by the British government. It is rumored that Anne's son went on to live a normal life, but no one can be sure if this is true or not.

After being found guilty of piracy, Anne Bonny confessed that she had wanted Calico Jack dead so they could be together.

SHE WAS PREGNANT WITH their son, Morgan, who would later also become an infamous pirate. Her confession was used as an excuse for her release from prison by the governor of Jamaica.

While some historians have argued that the two women were executed after giving birth in prison, there are no records of this happening.

IT IS POSSIBLE THAT they were freed at some point and rejoined their families. Alternatively, they may have been pardoned and released from prison after giving birth, or pardoned and allowed to return home with their children.

Anne Bonny and Mary Read were two of the best-known pirates of the Golden Age of Piracy. Anne Bonny was born in Ireland and moved to South Carolina, where she married a sailor named James Bonny. She left her husband to join her lover onboard a pirate ship. They were both captured by a British warship, but they jumped overboard before they could be sent back to jail.

Mary Read was born in England and disguised herself as a man so that she could join her husband's pirate crew, who had been on land for several years without seeing each other due to his naval duties. They fought against each other during one battle and died together in combat on their ship "The Ranger" when an enemy cannonball hit them directly leaving no remains behind except for pieces of clothing scattered around their bodies which were found floating nearby later that day when someone noticed some blood stains on deck after hearing screams coming from below deck; however, these accounts may have been exaggerated since there are no records stating how exactly how these two women died nor do we know for sure if they ever met each other while alive."

Anne Bonny is one of the most famous pirates on record.

ANNE BONNY WAS AN IRISH pirate, born in 1690. She is one of the most famous pirates on record, and her story has been told in many different ways by many different authors, but what's clear is that she was a woman who defied gender roles and became captain of her own ship.

Anne Bonny was a pirate who captivated people with her story. Though she and Mary Read were two of the best-known pirates of the Golden Age of Piracy, they are also among the least well understood. For decades, historians have struggled to piece together what happened to these women after they were captured by Governor Woodes Rogers in 1720. We still don't know for sure - but this lack of certainty only makes their lives more interesting.

CHAPTER EIGHT HAYREDDIN BARBAROSSA

Hayreddin Barbarossa was born between 1466 and 1478 in the town of Karaman in Anatolia. His mother died when he was young and his father died when he was around 11 years old. After his father's death, his uncle took him to Istanbul. There he was trained in the same trade as that of his father. He served a number of years in the galleys under various commanders before being appointed to command a ship by Sultan Bayezid II in 1503.

Hayreddin Barbarossa, also known as Hızır Hayrettin Pasha, and Khair ad Din Pasha (1466/1478 - 4 July 1546), was an Ottoman corsair and later admiral of the Ottoman Navy. He became the first Bey (Governor) of Algiers, but was later removed by the Ottoman sultan for abusing his power. Barbarossa's naval victories secured Ottoman dominance over the Mediterranean during the mid 16th century.

HAYREDDIN WAS BORN in Anatolia, now part of Turkey to a family who were Turkish Beyliks and had risen to prominence under Osman I.[1] His father's name was Kara Ali Agha and his mother's name was Hayme Hatun. [2] The Turkish word "Beylik" means feudal fiefdom or principality [3], so in English language sources it is usually translated as "principality". The family had been established since at least 1291 and as early as 1423 had become hereditary governors of Sinop on behalf of their master Sultan Süleyman Çelebi.[4]

Barbarossa spent his childhood years in Karaman where he learned seamanship from a certain Maktoob ibn Abdullah Allami (known simply as Maktoob). A member of a wealthy merchant family with strong trade links at Constantinople[5], Maktoob ibn Abdullah Allami taught him to navigate by using instruments such as quadrante[6] and astrolabe[7]. Barbarossa soon mastered this skill and started sailing on trade routes between North Africa (notably Tunis)[8] or Egypt[9] on one hand while working closely with some leading local families on the other hand called "Aghas". This position allowed him access to highly profitable cargoes like gold dust from sub-Saharan mines which sometimes reached prices up 300 times higher than normal rates!

His mother died when he was young and his father died when he was around 11 years old.

HE HAD A DIFFICULT childhood because he had to fend for himself as a child. He had to learn how to survive on his own.

After his father's death, his uncle took him to

Istanbul. There he was trained in the same trade as that of his father.

AT THIS TIME, HAYREDDIN worked for a man named Selman Reis who was the chief admiral of Sultan Süleyman I (the Magnificent).

While working for Selman Reis, Hayreddin took part in many battles against pirates and captured many enemy ships. When he was 23 years old, he became a captain of a ship named 'Tekirdağ' which led other ships as well.

He served a number of years in the galleys under various commanders before being appointed to command a ship by Sultan Bayezid II in 1503.

HE WAS BORN IN 1466 or 1478, the son of a fisherman and part-time pirate. He was trained in his father's trade, serving as an oarsman on galleys under various commanders before being appointed to command a ship by Sultan Bayezid II in 1503.

Barbarossa became the most successful corsair of the sixteenth century, raiding Christian ships and towns along the Mediterranean Sea. By 1512 he had captured several islands for Islam and become known as Hayreddin "Barbarossa" – meaning Redbeard – for his red beard (which may have been dyed). He was awarded command over all Ottoman naval forces after helping to defeat Spanish forces at Tunis in 1535.

After Sultan Selim I died in 1520 getting into a fight with Safiye over who should have control of Algiers, Barbarossa was made Admiral-in-Chief of all Turkish fleets in the West Mediterranean Sea; however, when Safiye finally gained complete control over Selim's successor Süleyman I (reigned 1520–66), she dismissed him from this post and sent him back to Algiers in disgrace.

IN CONCLUSION, BARBAROSSA was one of the greatest pirates in history. He was able to fight off many enemies and even capture some of their ships.

CHAPTER NINE BARTHOLOMEW ROBERTS AKA BLACK BART

The name Bart Roberts has long been synonymous with the Golden Age of Piracy. His exploits against Spanish ships have made him an icon in popular culture and his legend grew even more when he was killed by his own men after being wounded in battle.

Bartholomew Roberts, pirate captain of the ship known as The Royal Fortune, was born in Wales in 1682 or 1683. He was born John Roberts and later changed his name to Bartholomew. Roberts was born in Swansea, a small town called Kidwelly located near Cardiff. He was the youngest of 12 children; his father had died two years before his birth and his mother remarried twice after that leaving him to fend for himself at an early age.

He became apprenticed to a tailor during this time but left after three years due to disagreements with his master over finances and began working as a sailor on merchant ships out of Bristol where he learned navigation skills that would come in handy later on during his pirating career.

Roberts had many nicknames during his career as a pirate including: "Black Bart"; "Barti Ddu Fach" (Welsh for "Little Bart the Small"); "Old Black"; "The Welsh Captain"; "The Red Rover"; and most famously, "Black Bart".

He had a privateering commission.

A PRIVATEER WAS A LICENSED ship owner who had permission from the government to attack and capture enemy ships. Although privateers would sometimes steal booty from the captured ships, they were not pirates because they were authorized by their governments.

Privateering commissions were issued by countries at war, authorizing merchants to arm their own vessels with cannons and crew them with men not already serving in the regular navy. Privateers could be hired by anyone—even pirates—and offered a quick way for merchants without access to official navies or naval forces to harass their enemies' shipping lanes. In addition to England and France, many other European nations issued privateering commissions during this period (including Spain) but it was the British who had most success using this method during the wars against France between 1689 and 1713 (known as Queen Anne's War).

He captured more than 430 ships during his career.

HE IS WELL KNOWN FOR his sense of style and fashion. He had a privateering commission.

Some historians believe that Roberts was born in Wales in 1682 or 1683, but others say he was born in Bristol, England. It's also possible that he was born in the Channel Islands (which belong to Great Britain) or Cornwall (which belongs to England).

He died in combat.

IN APRIL OF 1722, ROBERTS was in a battle with the British navy. During the fighting, he was killed by a shot to his head. His body was thrown overboard along with two other pirates who died alongside him. Their bodies were buried at sea and their ships were destroyed by cannon fire by British sailors.

It is believed that before embarking on a life of piracy, he was a slave trader.

He was known for his sense of style and fashion.

- Black Bart was known for his sense of style and fashion.

- He was known to wear a red velvet coat, which was very fashionable at the time.

- His hat was also very fashionable, but it might have been more important than just being stylish or fashionable. It helped protect him from sunburn and other skin problems that can occur during long hours on a ship. The Caribbean sun is intense and can cause serious damage if it isn't kept away with some kind of covering.

THE GOLD RINGS HE WORE on his fingers showed everyone who saw him that he had been successful in his journey as a pirate captain; this would help bring respect from those who knew of him and feared him as well as attract new recruits to join his crew because they wanted to be part of something that seemed successful.

WHILE POSING AS A DUTCH merchant vessel called the Princess, Roberts captured two French brigs and another Dutch ship. The ships were renamed the Royal Fortune, the Good Hope, and the Ranger.

That same year he took a Portuguese galleon called Nuestra Señora de la Concepción with 500 slaves on board (the largest prize ever taken by one pirate in history). This gave him his next three names: Black Bart for his appearance, Bartholomew for his original name, and John Roberts for his son's middle name.

On January 10, 1722 he captured his most famous prize — the 40-gun Portuguese frigate Santa Catherina. Roberts' crew renamed her the Royal Fortune.

ROBERTS WAS A MASTER of strategy, who used every trick in the book to outwit his enemies and achieve victory. He was also a daring sailor who never hesitated to risk everything for one last shot at glory and riches. Once on top of an enemy ship, he would storm into their gun deck with a pistol in each hand, shouting: "Come on board you scurvy dogs! We are ready for you!"

Roberts' greatest claim to fame came when he took over two ships loaded with valuables from Rio de Janeiro after capturing them off Cape Lopez (Angola). The two ships were known as HMS Swallow and HMS Weymouth; both were heavily armed English warships under Captain Chaloner Whitmore who had been sent by Vice Admiral Sir Henry Jennings aboard HMS Ruby (a third vessel) following reports that Roberts had been seen off Africa's coast near Sierra Leone."

He was one of the most successful pirates ever.

AS A PIRATE, ROBERTS is credited with the capture of over 430 ships. This makes him one of the most successful pirates in history.

I learned a lot about the man who would become Black Bart, and I hope that you have enjoyed reading it as much as I did during the researching process.

CHAPTER TEN ROBERTO CONFRESI

Born in 1791 in Santa Cruz de Tenerife, Canary Islands. He was born as the son of an Irish father and Spanish mother. Roberto Cofresi Ramirez Machay was also known as El Pirata Cofresí. After receiving his primary education, he joined the Navy of Spain where he learned navigation and other skills while working under his uncle who was also a captain of a ship. From there he went on to become one of the most famous pirates and privateers that ever lived.

He lived on a small island called Vieques off Puerto Rico with his mother and father. His father was a fisherman and his mother was a housewife.

Roberto grew up as an orphan because he lost both parents at an early age due to plague which swept through his small island home leaving no one alive except himself and one other boy named Juan de la Cruz who later became known as El Conde del Guajiro (the count of Gaojiro).

At this point in time there were many pirates operating in this region due to smuggling activities between Cuba and Puerto Rico being one of them Roberto decided to take up piracy too so he could get some money for himself since he had no family left behind after their deaths from plague including grandparents whom were also dead at another place altogether called Santa Catalina Island which is close by Vieques Island where they used live earlier before moving out onto mainland Puerto Rico.

Age: 30 Years old.

ROBERTO COFRESI, ALSO known as "El Pirata Cofresí" (The Pirate Roberto), was 30 years old when he died. He had already been around the Caribbean for almost 15 years. If you want to know more about the famous pirate, Roberto Cofresí is said to have had long brown hair and blue eyes; he was tall for his time period at 1m82 (5 ft 11in).

ROBERTO WAS KNOWN AS El Pirata Cofresí (the Pirate of Cofresi). He fought against the Spanish government and defended the freedom of trade with Puerto Rico by attacking Spanish ships that traded with other countries without permission from the local authorities.

His profession was captain of the ship, privateer, and slave trader.

A pirate is a person who attacks ships for money while a privateer is authorized by a government to attack non-enemy ships as part of its navy. The privateers were paid well for their service in exchange for attacking enemy ships, so they could afford better equipment than pirates did. Slave traders captured Africans and sold them as slaves in other countries or islands such as Cuba and Puerto Rico.

- **Religion and ideology: Catholic, and Freemason.**

- **Roberto Cofresí was the son of Juan and María de los Dolores Prieto. His parents were farmers who lived in Santa Cruz de Tenerife, Canary Islands. Juan was also a captain at sea during the second half of the 17th century. The pirate's parents died when he was young which led him to live with his uncle Diego Prieto y Pérez de Guzmán (who is also mentioned as his godfather).**

● Cofresí studied with José Ignacio Márquez y Rodríguez and learned Latin grammar at nighttime classes taught by Sebastián de Mejía e Ibarrola after being expelled from school due to his bad behavior (he would have been about 12 years old). He was said to be an extremely intelligent boy who had plenty of free time due to his father dying when he was a child; he used this as an opportunity for self-improvement by studying languages such as Italian, English, French and German which made him a great conversationalist later on in life.

Roberto Cofresí was also a revolutionary, a poet and an artist. He was also a privateer and he used this power to become one of the most powerful pirates in history, leading attacks on over 100 ships in his lifetime.

Cofresí spent most of his life as an outlaw but ended up doing something pretty interesting: he created artworks out of gold and silver coins that he stole from his victims' ships.

● Roberto Cofresí was born in Puerto Rico, on March 23, 1791. His father was a Spanish military officer for a time and his mother was a common Spanish woman. He had three brothers and two sisters.

● The year he turned one, El Pirata Cofresí's family moved to Santo Domingo where his father served as commander of the naval port of Santo Domingo until 1808 when he died during an epidemic disease outbreak among troops (typhus) and the locals. At this point, Roberto was orphaned by both parents.

Place of death of Roberto Cofresí (March 29, 1825).

ROBERTO WAS SENTENCED to death by hanging, and he was executed on March 29, 1825. His body was buried in a mass grave. The head was put on display on the wall of Fort San Felipe del Morro.

In English: Roberto Cofresí (1790-1825) was a famous Puerto Rican pirate who terrorized the Caribbean during his career as a privateer employed by the

Spanish government to defend their colonies from piracy. However, he later turned to piracy himself and became known as El Pirata Cofresí. It is said that he was responsible for causing more than two thousand deaths between 1817 and 1825 alone!

In Spanish: Roberto Cofresi Ramirez Machay (1790-1825), el pirata conocido como "El Pirata Cofresi" fue un famoso pirata puertorriqueño que atemorizó al Caribe durante su carrera como corsario empleado por la Corona Española para defender sus colonias contra los corsarios piratas enemigos de España. No obstante, él también se convirtió en un corsario y se convertiría en uno de los piratas más feroces del Caribe; ya que se dice que causó más de 2 mil muertes entre 1817 y 1825 solamente!

THE LIFE OF ROBERTO Cofresí was an example of courage, bravery, and honor. From his early childhood, he knew how to live with dignity and respect. His desire to fight for freedom led him to become a pirate, and he eventually became one of the most famous outlaws in history. Today he is thought of as a kind of Robin Hood. He died at the age of 35 years by firing squad. He was considered by many as The Last of the West India pirates.

Don't miss out!

Visit the website below and you can sign up to receive emails whenever rodney cannon publishes a new book. There's no charge and no obligation.

https://books2read.com/r/B-A-YPE-EWBDC

BOOKS2READ

Connecting independent readers to independent writers.